What Is the Story of Batman™?

What Is the Story of Batman™?

by Michael Burgan

illustrated by Jake Murray

Penguin Workshop

To my father, who patiently took me to
an auto show when I was six years old, just
so I could see the Batmobile—MB

Dedicated to the first conversation I ever had with
my wife, where we agreed that *The Dark Knight*
was a pretty awesome movie—JM

PENGUIN WORKSHOP
An Imprint of Penguin Random House LLC, New York

If you purchased this book without a cover, you should be aware that this book is stolen
property. It was reported as "unsold and destroyed" to the publisher, and neither the author
nor the publisher has received any payment for this "stripped book."

Penguin supports copyright. Copyright fuels creativity, encourages diverse voices, promotes
free speech, and creates a vibrant culture. Thank you for buying an authorized edition
of this book and for complying with copyright laws by not reproducing, scanning,
or distributing any part of it in any form without permission. You are supporting writers
and allowing Penguin to continue to publish books for every reader.

The publisher does not have any control over and does not assume any responsibility
for author or third-party websites or their content.

Published by Penguin Workshop, an imprint of Penguin Random House LLC, New York.
PENGUIN and PENGUIN WORKSHOP are trademarks of Penguin Books Ltd.
WHO HQ & Design is a registered trademark of Penguin Random House LLC.
Printed in the USA.

Visit us online at www.penguinrandomhouse.com.

Library of Congress Control Number: 2019034749

ISBN 9781524788339 (paperback)   10 9 8 7 6 5 4 3 2 1
ISBN 9781524788346 (library binding)   10 9 8 7 6 5 4 3 2 1

Contents

What Is the Story of Batman?

In 1939, comic book fans across the United States met a new super hero. When they picked up the May issue of *Detective Comics*, they saw someone called the Bat-Man on the cover. He wore a black mask and a cape that opened like a pair of bat wings. Who was Batman? Readers soon found out.

In *Detective Comics No. 27*, Batman's story was called "The Case of the Chemical Syndicate." His name was written as "The Bat-Man." In it, Batman searches for clues to solve a crime. Along the way, he goes after the bad guys. He knocks one out with a single punch. Batman picks up another and tosses him over his shoulder! Using his brains and his great strength, Batman solves the case.

Batman appeared in other issues of *Detective Comics*. The super hero tracked down and captured all sorts of criminals. His belt held tools that helped him fight crime, including a rope Batman used to swing from one rooftop to another.

More comic book readers became Batman fans, and in 1940, he became the star of his own comic book. It was titled simply *Batman*, and it promised "all brand new adventures." By now, Batman had a young friend named Robin, who helped him fight crime. In that first issue of *Batman*, they are trying to catch the Joker. Batman and Robin track him down and arrest him. But the Joker is a clever criminal, and he manages to escape.

The Joker would become one of many villains Batman faced again and again.

Since the first Batman comic in 1939, millions of people around the world have come to love Batman. He's also sometimes called the Dark Knight and the Caped Crusader. Over the years, his costume has changed, and he has faced new villains. But fans know one thing is always true: Batman is a smart, strong, and complicated super hero who will always fight for justice.

CHAPTER 1
The Birth of Batman

As a child, Bob Kane eagerly read the comics in the newspaper. He loved to draw, and by the time he was in high school, he knew he wanted to be an artist. But not an artist who worked with paint, or turned clay or marble into sculptures. Bob Kane wanted to draw comic strips and create his own characters. And in 1938, he got the chance.

At the time, Bob was working for Detective Comics, which eventually would be known by the initials "DC." The company published several different comic book series. One was called *Action Comics*. In 1938, *Action* introduced the world's first super hero: Superman. The Man of Steel, as he is also known, is from a distant planet called Krypton. Bullets can't harm him. He uses his X-ray vision to see through walls, and he can fly. Superman also has another, more average, identity. When he's not catching criminals, he's a newspaper reporter named Clark Kent.

Superman and Clark Kent

Comic book fans in 1939 loved Superman. His success convinced DC Comics that it needed another super hero. A DC editor, Vin Sullivan, asked Bob if he wanted to try creating one. He quickly said yes. Leaving work on a Friday, he went home and spent the entire weekend developing his new character.

As he worked, Bob thought back to some drawings he had seen years before. The great Italian painter and inventor Leonardo da Vinci had sketched out ideas for early flying machines—hundreds of years before the first airplanes flew! One of his drawings showed a machine with large wings. Da Vinci never built flying machines that worked, but his sketches inspired Bob Kane. His new super hero would have wings, too.

Leonardo da Vinci

Bob drew wings like da Vinci's on the figure of a man. He thought of several different names for the character he created, such as hawk-man, eagle-man, and bird-man. Then in bigger letters, he wrote, "Bat-man?"

He also copied down some words da Vinci had once written as he studied the idea of human flight. Da Vinci had said that a bat would be the perfect model for learning how to fly. Just before he created Batman, Bob Kane dug his early drawings out of a trunk, where they had been stored for years. Seeing his old drawings again inspired Bob to create the Batman the world knows today.

Bob also thought of an old movie hero he had seen, called Zorro. On-screen, Zorro fought bad guys while wearing a black mask across his eyes. The mask helped to hide his real identity as a wealthy landowner named Don Diego. Bob decided to give his super hero a mask. Batman's identity would be a secret, too.

But the drawings of this new Batman were still not enough to launch a comic book. Bob needed someone to write stories for his super hero, so he turned to Bill Finger. Bill and Bob had worked together on other comics. Bob showed his partner the sketches of Batman, and Bill came up with a few suggestions. He thought Batman's costume should be mostly gray to create a feeling of mystery. He also thought Batman's mask should look even more like a bat's head than what Bob had originally sketched. He then suggested that Batman should not have actual wings, as the

Bill Finger

da Vinci flying machine did. Instead, he would have a cape that *looked* like bat wings, so that he could move around easily to fight criminals.

How Comic Books Are Created

It takes more than one person to create the finished look of a comic book. First, the artist prepares a layout, which shows the position of the different panels that fill one page. When the layout is done, the artist begins to draw the details of each panel in pencil.

At the next step, another artist goes over the pencil sketches in ink. Then color is added inside the lines by a colorist. Another person, called a letterer, fills in the balloons that contain the characters' words and descriptions of the action.

For the early Batman stories, one person might do more than one of these steps. An artist named Jerry Robinson, for example, did both lettering and background art. He also sometimes illustrated the covers for DC comic books.

On Monday morning, Bob showed his drawings of Batman to his editor, Vin Sullivan, who took them to his boss, Jack Liebowitz. As he said years later, Liebowitz didn't understand the idea of a crime fighter who dressed like a bat. But Superman had become so popular, DC Comics wanted to take a chance on a new super hero.

Batman's look was complete. Now Bill Finger had to write a few adventures for him. He thought of Batman as a brilliant detective who was also a skilled athlete and fighter. Unlike Superman, Batman was human. He did not have super powers. He could not fly or see through walls. And—because he was human—he could be wounded by bullets or hurt in a fight. Batman had to use his strength and smarts to defeat any bad guys he faced.

Batman made his first appearance in a comic book called *Detective Comics* dated May 1939.

The cover promised readers "the amazing and unique adventures of the Batman!" And comic book fans were delighted!

CHAPTER 2
The First Adventures

The very first Batman story, in *Detective Comics No. 27*, showed just how good he was at finding and capturing criminals. It also introduced readers to Commissioner James Gordon, the head of the local police. And, on the last page of the story, readers finally learned Batman's real identity:

Bruce Wayne

He is a millionaire named Bruce Wayne, who has decided to spend his life fighting crime. When the police can't solve a case, Batman can.

Commissioner Gordon and Bruce Wayne were friends, but the commissioner didn't know that his buddy was also Batman! As the story ended, readers learned that one person was both Wayne and Batman. But the police commissioner did not have a clue about Batman's true identity.

In the next Batman story, he begins to use one of the many tools that help him move through the city and fight crime. He takes a rope off his belt, throws it around a pole, and then swings away from police, who still aren't sure if Batman is a crime fighter or just another criminal.

Batman had a powerful swing: *Crash!* He had a powerful left punch: *Sock!* And a powerful right punch, too: *Crack!* The very last comic panel of the story states, "If the commissioner could see his young friend now . . . he'd be amazed to learn that he is The 'Bat-Man!' "

In one of the early stories, Batman drove a simple type of helicopter called a Bat-Gyro. A gyrocopter is an early form of helicopter that first flew during the 1920s. The Bat-Gyro had both wings like a plane and a rotating blade like a helicopter. Batman sometimes used it to stay high above the city and do his crime fighting from the air.

Bat-Gyro

In November 1939, readers learned why Bruce Wayne had chosen to become Batman. As a young boy, Bruce had gone to the movies with his parents. As they left the theater, a man approached and demanded that Mrs. Wayne hand over her necklace. Mr. Wayne tried to push away

the thief, who fired a gun. Young Bruce watched
with horror as both his mother and father fell to
the ground, dead.

His parents had been very wealthy. But that
didn't change the fact that Bruce was now alone.
He spent most of his time improving his mind
and body. He studied to become a scientist, but
he also spent hours lifting weights. He promised
himself that he would devote his life to fighting
crime.

But how could a wealthy young man who was

well known and who lived in a large mansion do that? Bruce decided to hide his real identity. He needed to be something more mysterious and clever than the polite gentleman he really was. Just then, a bat flew in through an open window. In that instant, Bruce knew what to do: He would become Batman!

By 1940, Bob Kane wondered if something might be missing from the Batman stories. When he was a boy, he would sometimes pretend to go on adventures with the heroes he saw in the movies. Bob believed Batman's young readers might imagine themselves in the story. Working with Bill Finger, he decided to create a young super hero to fight alongside Batman, someone close to the readers' age, who would be a partner working with the Caped Crusader. In April 1940, Batman's young friend, Robin, appeared for the first time. His nickname was "the Boy Wonder."

Like Batman, Robin's costume hides his real
identity: Dick Grayson. And like Bruce Wayne,
Dick had become an orphan after his parents'
deaths. Bruce Wayne had offered to raise Dick

at his home, Wayne Manor. Dick soon found out that Bruce was actually Batman. Together, Batman and Robin are called the Dynamic Duo.

A Super Hero's Best Friend

When Robin entered Batman's world, he became the first comic book super hero teenage sidekick (usually a younger person who works with the main hero).

Dick Grayson was the first character to take the name Robin and help Batman fight crime. The next Robin was Jason Todd, who appeared in 1983. Other Robins after him were Tim Drake, Carrie Kelley (the first female Robin in the printed comic books), Stephanie Brown, and Damian Wayne. In 2014, Batman was briefly paired with a new sidekick—Bluebird, whose real identity was Harper Row.

Interestingly, Bob Kane had his own young "sidekick" at the time he created Robin. A seventeen-year-old college student named Jerry Robinson helped Kane draw Batman's stories.

Dick Grayson

Jason Todd

Damian Wayne

Tim Drake

Carrie Kelley

Bluebird

Comic books like *Detective Comics* usually featured a few different characters, each with their own separate stories, in one book. In the spring of 1940, Batman appeared in his very own comic book for the first time. Batman was a hit with readers! In the stories in *Batman No. 1*, the Caped Crusader and Robin battled

three criminals. And it included, once again, the details of how Bruce Wayne became Batman. While Batman now had his own comic book, he also still appeared in *Detective* and other DC comic books.

The drawings in the first Batman stories suggested that he lived and worked in New

York City. But by the end of 1940, Batman's fans discovered the true name of the city where Batman waged his crusade against crime. Batman's hometown was called Gotham City.

Batman and Robin lived in Wayne Manor. From the outside, it looked like a millionaire's beautiful estate. But beneath it was the Batcave. This was a secret space where Batman and Robin could design and build the cool gadgets and tools they used to catch the bad guys—the criminals who lived in Gotham City.

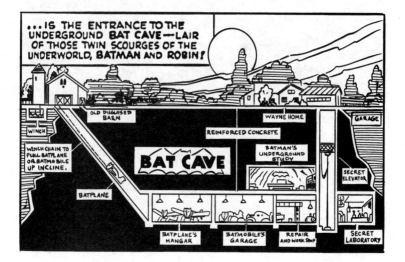

In 1941, the first real Batmobile that looked like the one fans know today appeared in *Batman No. 5*. It had a fin in the back and a bat-shaped figure on its hood. Of all the vehicles Batman used,

his specially made Batmobile became the most famous. Batman stored his car and his plane in the Batcave. The cave was an important place for Batman. It contained his garage, his office, and his scientific laboratory.

CHAPTER 3
The Villains

At first, Commissioner Gordon and the people of Gotham City weren't really sure if Batman was a good guy or a mysterious criminal. He seemed to show up everywhere the bad guys were! By the end of 1941, though, there was no question that Batman was a hero. Gordon had made Batman an honorary member of his police force. Everyone realized that Batman would be there to help the police fight crime.

When Gordon needed Batman's help, he turned on the Bat-Signal. The signal came from a large searchlight on the roof of the Gotham City police headquarters. The light projected the image of a bat in the sky.

PERHAPS THIS COMES A LITTLE LATE, BUT I, THE POLICE COMMISSIONER OF GOTHAM CITY, APPOINT YOU AN HONORARY MEMBER OF THE POLICE DEPARTMENT! FROM NOW ON, YOU WORK HAND IN HAND WITH THE POLICE!

THANK YOU, SIR! I WISH NOW THAT I COULD FIND THE PROOF THAT WILL PROVE BRUCE WAYNE'S INNOCENCE!

WHY, YOU SQUEALING RAT---I'LL KILL YA!

YOU'RE TOO LATE—HILL..... I'M DYING NOW, BUT AT LEAST I'M EVEN--- YOU----

THE BATMA HELPE. ME ESC: HE KEPT ME IN HIDEOL UNTIL I WAS

The Bat-Signal

The police used the Bat-Signal often, since Gotham City had its share of thieves and bad guys.

The most well-known Batman villain today is the Joker. He first appeared in *Batman No. 1*, looking like the joker from a deck of cards— but not in a fun way. Along with committing crimes, he loved playing pranks and practical jokes. The Joker also copied Batman's vehicles and tools. He built his own Jokermobile and utility belt. But instead of holding tools to fight crime, the Joker's belt held tricks and novelties including sneezing powder, itching powder, and a hand buzzer.

THE JOKER'S UTILITY BELT

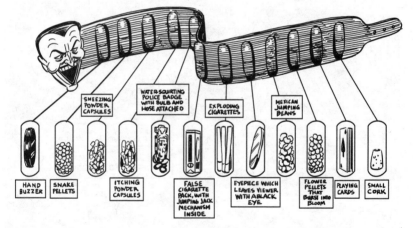

SNEEZING POWDER CAPSULES

WATER-SQUIRTING POLICE BADGE WITH BULB AND HOSE ATTACHED

EXPLODING CIGARETTES

MEXICAN JUMPING BEANS

HAND BUZZER | SNAKE PELLETS

ITCHING POWDER CAPSULES

FALSE CIGARETTE PACK, WITH JUMPING JACK MECHANISM INSIDE

EYEPIECE WHICH LEAVES VIEWER WITH A BLACK EYE

FLOWER PELLETS THAT BURST INTO BLOOM | PLAYING CARDS | SMALL CORK

It took years for readers to learn the Joker's origin story. A criminal using the name "Red Hood" led his gang to a factory. Batman and

Robin chased them there, where Red Hood fell into a huge vat of chemicals. Red Hood escaped. But the chemicals made his hair turn green, his lips very red, and his skin chalky white. He looked like an evil clown, and he began calling himself the Joker.

Catwoman

Selina Kyle without her disguise

Along with the Joker, *Batman No. 1* introduced a villain known as the Cat. She appeared again in the next issue as Catwoman. Her real identity is Selina Kyle. She was a jewel thief who at first disguised herself as an old woman.

What Is an Origin Story?

We often meet characters—especially in comic books—in the middle of the story or an exciting adventure. To help readers understand the characters better, writers often later provide what is called their origin story. This includes a history of the character that helps readers to know why they do what they do. The origin story might be about the character's childhood. Or it might tell of an event that has shaped the character's behavior and identity.

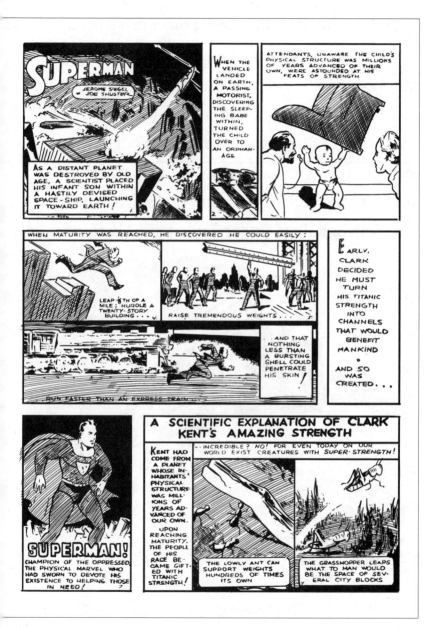

SUPERMAN

JEROME SIEGEL
JOE SHUSTER

As a distant planet was destroyed by old age, a scientist placed his infant son within a hastily devised space-ship, launching it toward Earth!

When the vehicle landed on Earth, a passing motorist, discovering the sleeping babe within, turned the child over to an orphanage.

Attendants, unaware the child's physical structure was millions of years advanced of their own, were astounded at his feats of strength.

When maturity was reached, he discovered he could easily:

Leap 1/8th of a mile; hurdle a twenty-story building . . . .

Raise tremendous weights . . .

Run faster than an express train . . . .

. . . and that nothing less than a bursting shell could penetrate his skin!

Early, Clark decided he must turn his titanic strength into channels that would benefit mankind

•

And so was created . . .

SUPERMAN!

Champion of the oppressed, the physical marvel who had sworn to devote his existence to helping those in need!

A SCIENTIFIC EXPLANATION OF CLARK KENT'S AMAZING STRENGTH

Kent had come from a planet whose inhabitants' physical structure was millions of years advanced of our own. Upon reaching maturity, the people of his race became gifted with titanic strength!

--Incredible? No! For even today on our world exist creatures with super-strength!

The lowly ant can support weights hundreds of times its own

The grasshopper leaps what to man would be the space of several city blocks

As Catwoman, Selina wore a mask that covered her eyes and had cat ears. During her life of crime, she also copied some of Batman's best ideas. She got a "Kitty Car" that had a large cat's head on the hood and cat's paws that stretched out next to the front tires. (It was later called the Catmobile.) She also had special gloves with claws that helped her climb buildings, just as Batman used his rope.

Kitty Car

In 1941, Batman met the Scarecrow for the first time. The Scarecrow had once been a professor named Jonathan Crane. He was an expert in what scared people. He lost his teaching job because he demonstrated his ideas in the classroom. Years later, as the Scarecrow, he invented a chemical that would make a person's deepest fears seem real enough to frighten them. His knowledge of chemistry and his great intelligence made the Scarecrow a serious problem for Batman and the people of Gotham City.

At the end of 1941, the Penguin made his first appearance in a Batman comic book. His real name is Oswald Chesterfield Cobblepot. Like Bruce Wayne, he came from a wealthy family. But after being teased as a child because he was short and round, Cobblepot became filled with anger. When he grew up, he used the name the Penguin. He wore a top hat and a tuxedo. The fancy suit made him look a little like a black-and-white bird. But he was just another bad guy. The Penguin always carried an umbrella, and many of them turned out to be weapons that could release poison gas or shoot flames. One had blades that spun like a helicopter, helping the Penguin to escape up and away.

Soon after Batman first met the Penguin, he confronted a villain called Two-Face. His real identity was Harvey Kent (though in later stories his last name is Dent, and that's how most Batman fans know him today). Dent was a successful lawyer. He was famous for his good looks. But Dent's life changed forever after the left side of his handsome face was burned with acid. With his looks ruined, the good-guy lawyer turned into the bad guy Two-Face.

Two-Face could choose to show his handsome side or his scarred left side. He was not evil all the time. He knew that breaking the law was wrong. When he felt like committing a crime, he flipped a silver dollar into the air. But instead of having a heads side and a tails side, his coin had heads on both sides. On one, the face looks normal. On the other, it has a scar. When the scary side of the coin turned up, Two-Face did exactly as he pleased, and he broke the law.

With a growing list of bad guys to fight, Batman was one busy super hero! And each month, DC Comics fans couldn't wait for the latest edition of *Batman*.

CHAPTER 4
A Popular Super Hero

For a time, Robin was the only person who knew Batman's real identity, but that changed in 1943. In *Batman No. 16*, Alfred Pennyworth arrived at Wayne Manor. Alfred's father had once worked as the Wayne family's butler,

taking care of the large home. Now Alfred would do the same for Bruce Wayne. Soon, though, he became much more than a butler. Alfred discovered that Bruce and Dick were Batman and Robin, and he became a key part of their crime-fighting team.

MOMENTS LATER, THE BATPLANE RACES THROUGH THE NIGHT SKY...

AND AS THE DARING HEROES KEEP ANOTHER RENDEZVOUS WITH HIGH ADVENTURE, ALFRED MAKES A COMPROMISE WITH HIS CONSCIENCE!

THEY ARE SO IMPRESSED WITH ME, IT WOULD NEVER DO TO TELL THEM I LEARNED THEIR IDENTITY BY SHEER LUCK! MUCH BETTER TO ACT MYSTERIOUS AND SAY NOTHING!

ALFRED CAN BE USEFUL, AT THAT! HE SAVED OUR LIVES IN THE THEATER! HE MUST BE SMARTER THAN WE THINK TO HAVE SEEN THROUGH OUR DISGUISE!

KEEP AN EYE ON ALFRED! YOU HAVEN'T SEEN THE LAST OF HIM!

The idea that Bruce Wayne should have a
butler came from the people who made the first
film version of the Batman comics. The butler
in the film was thin and had a mustache. DC
Comics writer Don Cameron had made Alfred
short and plump. And his last name was Beagle.
Soon after, the comics caught up to the movie,

and Alfred's look and name were sealed in
Batman history.

During the summer of 1943, Batman and
Robin appeared in a movie serial—a series of short
films—that lasted for fifteen weeks. Serials played
at movie theaters before the longer feature film.
One story continued over many short episodes.

Batman's Trusted Butler

Alfred Pennyworth has a wide range of duties working for the Caped Crusader. In addition to keeping the secret of Batman's true identity, he treats wounds and repairs Batman's suit when it's damaged. Alfred sometimes helps Batman and Robin fight crime. Stories of Alfred's own adventures appeared in the back of Batman comics for many years.

Alfred remains a key character in Batman's stories. In 2018, the television network Epix announced that it was developing a television series about Alfred. In this story, Alfred is a former special-forces soldier, played by Jack Bannon, who works with Bruce Wayne's father in the years before Bruce is even born.

Jack Bannon as young Alfred in the new series *Pennyworth*

That same year, Batman and Robin became the stars of their own daily newspaper comic strip. During the week, the strips were in black-and-white, but the Sunday comics were in full color. Bob Kane did the artwork for the daily strips, and many of the DC Comics writers created the stories. The comic strips ended in 1946. By then, Batman was on radio, too, fighting the same villains he battled in his comic books.

As Batman's adventures continued, Bob Kane and Bill Finger tried to put their super hero in different kinds of stories. At times, Batman and Robin traveled back in time and met famous historical figures, such as Bob's hero, Leonardo da Vinci. In another story, Batman ends up on another planet, and the people who live there make him their king!

Bob and Bill also created a new villain. The

Riddler was introduced in 1948. He always left riddles as clues at the scene of a crime. He was challenging Batman to solve puzzles to find him. Over time, the Riddler became one of the most well-known villains in the Batman stories.

More new characters entered Batman's world during the 1950s. He and Robin got a pet in 1955—a German shepherd named Ace, who was also called Bat-Hound. Ace wore a mask, just like his owner. He used his keen sense of smell to track down criminals.

The Batman family continued to grow. In 1956, Batwoman appeared. Her real identity was Kathy Kane. She was trained as a circus acrobat and wanted to fight crime like her hero, Batman. In her first story, Batwoman makes her own bat costume and drives a Batcycle. This motorcycle is so fast it can outrun the Batmobile. Batwoman at first battles criminals on her own, but then she teams up with Batman and Robin. In 1961, Kathy Kane's niece, Betty Kane, appeared as Bat-Girl, the sidekick to her aunt, Batwoman.

Bat-Girl

Batwoman

In 1960, DC brought a group of their super heroes together to form the Justice League of America (JLA). Batman continued to appear in his own comic books, but he was now a member of the JLA.

In 1964, a DC editor named Julius Schwartz teamed up with artist Carmine Infantino to give Batman a new look—more like a real person and less like a cartoon figure. The Caped Crusader now wore a yellow oval on his chest, with a bat inside it. The image looked just like the Bat-Signal.

The Justice League of America

With the Justice League of America, DC Comics created a team of super heroes. They were "foes of evil!" and "enemies of injustice!" Joining Batman on the team were Superman, Wonder Woman, The Flash, Aquaman, Green Lantern, and Martian Manhunter.

The JLA first appeared in a DC comic book

Green Lantern

Martian Manhunter

Flash

Superman

called *The Brave and the Bold*, but the team soon had its own comic book. The origin story for the JLA describes how they all came together to fight aliens battling one another for control of Earth. When the seven successfully defeat the aliens, they decide to form their league. Over the years, some members of the league have changed. New members have included Cyborg, the Atom, and Starfire. Today the team is known simply as the Justice League.

Wonder
Woman

Batman

Aquaman

The yellow oval came to symbolize Batman, just like the yellow diamond on his chest did for Superman. But another big change for Batman was still ahead.

Was the World's Greatest Detective ready for television?

CHAPTER 5
Batman Comes to Television

By the mid-1960s, television had replaced radio as the most popular form of home entertainment. In 1965, almost every US home had at least one set. Many children had stopped reading comics because they could watch cartoons and other shows for kids on TV. The ABC television network thought children might be excited to watch a show about one of the greatest comic super heroes. ABC decided to give Batman his own show.

Batman first aired in January 1966. The show ran on two different nights each week. The first episode ended with what's called a cliffhanger— a suspenseful moment that left fans wondering how the show would end. Batman and Robin were usually in great danger at the end of the first show. Viewers had to watch the week's second episode to learn how they escaped and then caught the criminal.

Adam West as Batman

Batman was a huge hit! The first two episodes were among the ten most-watched shows in America that week, and the next two were even more popular. The show starred Adam West as Batman and Burt Ward as Robin. Just as in the comics, they lived in Wayne Manor, over the

Batcave, and they drove in the Batmobile. Alfred was always there to help them, and the Dynamic Duo were called into action whenever they saw the Bat-Signal.

During the second season of the show, DC introduced a new version of the Batgirl character who was the daughter of Commissioner Gordon. Barbara Gordon, as Batgirl, would soon thereafter also begin to appear in *Batman* on television.

The first villain Batman and Robin faced in the new show was the Riddler—one of the biggest criminals in Gotham City. Others who appeared often on the show were the Joker, the Penguin, and Catwoman. These four villains also teamed up against Batman in a movie that was based on the TV show. *Batman*, the movie, was released later in 1966 and was the first full-length Batman movie. The actors who appeared in the TV show also starred in the movie.

Working with DC, the writers of the *Batman*

Villains from the 1966 *Batman* movie

show created some new super villains who had never appeared in Batman comics. One was called Egghead. He had a bald head and wore a white-and-yellow suit. Egghead believed he was the world's smartest criminal. Another was the Bookworm, who loved to read. He wore thick glasses and a leather suit. Both later appeared in the comic stories as well.

Egghead

With the show's success, toy companies began to produce many different Batman toys and other items. Kids could wear their own utility belt, with a Batarang (a bat-shaped boomerang) and Batrope.

The First Real Batmobile

Before Batman appeared on television, his special car was just a drawing on a page. The makers of the *Batman* TV show needed a real Batmobile, and Barris Kustom Industries created it.

In 1955, the Ford Motor Company unveiled an automobile to show people what cars of the future might look like. It was called the Lincoln Futura and it cost $250,000 to build! Several years later,

Ford sold it to George Barris for just $1. Barris had a business that took old cars and made them look new. He also sometimes added new features to cars, so they looked much different than they originally had. For the Batmobile, Barris customized the Futura to look more bat-like and painted it black. Barris made three more Batmobiles that looked just like the original. He kept the first one he made, and in 2013 it sold at an auction for over $4 million!

They could also buy Batman and Robin costumes to wear on Halloween. There was even a Batman puppet theater, with hand puppets of the Dynamic Duo and the Joker.

By its third season, *Batman* was not as popular as it once had been. Some of the new villains were not as evil—or as funny—as the first ones. And not all the people who read Batman comics were fans of the show. They thought the program made fun of the super hero they loved. They didn't like the colorful costumes or the silliness of the writing, even though the sound effects from Batman's blows against the crooks were written in large letters, just as in the comics: *POW!* or *CRAACK!*

ABC began to air just one episode a week. And by March 1968, *Batman* the show was no longer on television.

But Batman didn't disappear from TV screens altogether. Just months after *Batman* ended, the CBS network began broadcasting a cartoon series called the *Batman/Superman Hour*. The show featured each super hero in his own stories.

Thanks in part to the success of the *Batman* TV show, sales of the comic books had soared. In 1966, DC sold an average of almost nine hundred thousand *Batman* comics per issue. That was almost double the copies sold the year before, and more than all the comics DC sold in 1939, the year Batman first appeared! Sales of *Batman* comics were strong again in 1967, when it was the top-selling comic book series in the United States.

CHAPTER 6
Batman's Changing World

Before the new animated series had even aired, there were changes at DC Comics. In 1967, Carmine Infantino began to play a larger role in the production of Batman and other comics. Shortly before, Bob Kane retired from the company. A new generation of artists and writers would try to keep the Caped Crusader popular with his millions of fans.

One of the major new DC artists was Neal Adams. In 1968, he drew a cover featuring Batman for a comic book in a series called *The Brave and the Bold.* By 1970, Adams was drawing full Batman stories for DC's *Detective Comics* and Batman's own books.

Neal Adams

In his work, Neal Adams often showed Batman in the dark or hidden in shadows. Adams and the writers he worked with wanted to leave behind the humor of the TV show and portray Batman as a serious crime fighter again.

Dennis O'Neil

One of those writers was Dennis O'Neil. He tried to bring a sense of mystery and chilling terror to Batman's adventures.

As the new team created new adventures for Batman, they brought back one of his old enemies. Harvey Dent, better known as

Two-Face, appeared in the comics for the first time in seventeen years. Adams and O'Neil also made the Joker more corrupt than he had been in years. He wasn't just a crook who liked to pull pranks. He was now a murderer, too.

Adams also helped introduce new villains to the Batman comic books. One of them was Man-Bat, who first appeared in 1970. Scientist Kirk Langstrom was trying to use real bats to create a chemical that would give him their sensitive hearing. Instead, the potion turned him into a creature that was half man and half bat. In his first story, Man-Bat helped Batman fight Gotham City's bad guys. But he soon turned into a villain himself.

Working with O'Neil in 1971, Adams also created Ra's al Ghul, a man who could live forever. His name is Arabic for "Demon's Head," and he had the fighting skills of a deadly killer. Ra's al Ghul believed

that humans were overcrowding the planet and destroying it with pollution. His answer to the problem, though, was not to help people clean up the earth. Instead, Ra's al Ghul thought people needed to be wiped out!

Unlike most other villains, Ra's al Ghul discovered that Batman and Bruce Wayne were the same person. He respected Batman's great detective skills. And he hoped Batman would one day lead the organization called the

Brotherhood of the Demon. Batman rejected the idea, of course, and he and Ra's al Ghul became enemies.

DC Comics gave its writers the freedom to present Batman in new ways, and sometimes their stories had new twists. In 1982, Batman faced a villain named the Monk, who had first appeared in a 1939 comic. The Monk is a vampire. He bites Batman and turns him into a vampire, too!

Batman must then get blood from the Monk to make himself human once again. In the end, Batman defeats the Monk and also saves himself.

By 1983, Dick Grayson, as Robin, had been spending more of his time as part of a group of young super heroes called the Teen Titans. Jason Todd came to live with Bruce Wayne and serve as his sidekick. As Robin, Jason helped Batman carry on his lifelong battle against crime in Gotham City. Dick Grayson now had a new super hero identity: Nightwing. And Batman was once again being called one of his old nicknames: the Dark Knight.

Nightwing

CHAPTER 7
The Dark Knight

In the very first issue of Batman's 1940 comic book, one of his nicknames had been the Dark Knight. The name never became as popular or widely used as the "Caped Crusader." But in 1986, artist and writer Frank Miller changed that.

Miller had been writing and drawing comics since the 1970s, when he first went to work at DC. He and one of the top editors at DC developed the idea for *Batman: The Dark Knight Returns*.

The story appeared over four issues. Miller wrote the books and did the penciling while Klaus Janson did the line inking. DC agreed to print the series on higher-quality paper than they used for other comics, so the color would look better. The books also had more pages than a typical Batman comic. *The Dark Knight Returns* became one of the most famous and best-selling comic book series of all time.

At the beginning of the story, Batman has stopped fighting crime in Gotham City. He's getting older, and criminals are ruining the city. Batman decides he must put on his cape and mask again and take on a gang called the Mutants. He also faces two of his old enemies: Two-Face and the Joker. And Batman now has a new Robin, a teenage girl named Carrie Kelley.

As Batman fights the Mutants, the people of Gotham City don't see him as the hero they once had. A new police commissioner thinks it's wrong for Batman to work on his own instead of letting the police keep the city safe. To try to stop Batman, the government sends Superman to Gotham to keep Batman off the streets.

In the last of the four issues, Batman and Superman fight each other! It seems as if Batman will defeat Superman. Batman actually pretends to die. He and Robin head to a remote cave and make plans for the future.

Frank Miller later said that his version of Batman had been a reaction to the 1960s TV show. Miller didn't want to joke about the super hero. Batman was a serious crime fighter dedicated to defeating evil. Miller went on to write several more stories about Batman. In 1987, he and artist David Mazzucchelli retold Batman's origin story—the events that led him to become a super hero. Their story—called *Batman: Year One*—appeared in four issues of the regular *Batman* comic, which were later bound into a single graphic novel.

Batman: Year One kept many of the details of the origin story Bob Kane and Bill Finger had created for Batman. But in Miller's tale, Batman has to battle some bad policemen in Gotham City as well as criminals. James Gordon is one of the good police officers, though at this point in his career he is not yet the police commissioner. Also appearing in the story are Alfred, Catwoman, and the lawyer Harvey Dent, who had not yet become the criminal Two-Face.

The success of Frank Miller's stories helped shape the first of an all-new series of Batman movies. His fans would soon see him on the big screen like never before.

From Comic Books to Graphic Novels

The Dark Knight Returns was so popular that in 1997, DC Comics combined the four issues into one book. It was an early example of what is today called a graphic novel. The term means different things to different people, and experts argue over what was the first graphic novel. But comic books clearly inspired this new graphic book format and style.

Graphic novels are usually longer than regular comic books and are printed on sturdier paper. Frank Miller's Batman graphic novel is still considered one of the best.

DC Comics had first used the term "graphic novel" in 1972 to describe a thirty-nine-page story called *The Sinister House of Secret Love No. 2*.

Will Eisner

In 1978, comic book writer and artist Will Eisner called one of his longer comic book stories a graphic novel. Some comic book fans have called Eisner the "father" of the graphic novel.

In 1969, DC Comics had become part of the same company that owned Warner Bros.—one of the oldest movie studios in America. In 1989, Warner Bros. released a new Batman movie.

The new movie was cast with well-known movie stars. Michael Keaton played Batman, and Jack Nicholson played the Joker. Tim Burton directed the movie. He had been influenced by both the original Batman stories of Bob Kane and Bill Finger and the Dark Knight stories of Frank Miller to create just the right look for this Batman. Many of the scenes took place at night, in the middle of dark city streets.

Jack Nicholson as the Joker and Michael Keaton as Batman.

In the movie, called simply *Batman*, the super hero does not wear gray tights, as he did in the comics at that time. Instead, he wears a black suit that looks almost like armor.

Robin does not appear in the film. Batman drives a new version of the Batmobile that was based in part on the Corvette Stingray of the 1950s.

Batmobile from the 1989 movie

In 1989, *Batman* made more money in the United States than any other movie. And just as the 1960s TV show led to new Batman products, so did the film. People once again bought toys

and clothing with the Batman symbol on them—
a black bat against a yellow oval background.
One company even sold Batman cereal, which
was advertised as having a "smashing taste!"

The success of *Batman* led to yet another movie in 1992. *Batman Returns* also starred Michael Keaton and was directed by Tim Burton. This time, Batman battles Catwoman, the Penguin, and a new villain named Max Shreck, a friend of the Penguin.

Batman returned to the big screen in 1995, in *Batman Forever*. Actor Val Kilmer took over the role of Batman, and Robin was played by Chris O'Donnell. They face the villains Two-Face and the Riddler. Two years later, *Batman and Robin* was released. It was the last Batman movie of the 1990s, with George Clooney playing Batman, O'Donnell as Robin, and Alicia Silverstone in the role of Batgirl. The three super heroes battle Mr. Freeze, Poison Ivy, and Bane.

New Batman Cartoons

While Warner Bros. was making new Batman movies, the Caped Crusader also returned to television. In 1992, the Fox Network began showing a cartoon series called *Batman: The Animated Series*. Artist Bruce Timm designed the characters. The new show appealed to both adults and kids. *Batman: The Animated Series* aired until 1995. It won several Emmys, which are the most important awards given to television shows in the United States.

In 1999, Timm began working on another animated Batman series, this time for Warner Bros.' own network. *Batman Beyond* is set in the future when Bruce Wayne, as an eighty-year-old man, is no longer fighting crime. He gives his Batsuit to a teenager named Terry McGinnis and teaches the teen his skills. Terry eventually gets a new suit with jets in its boots that allows him to fly! *Batman Beyond* ran for three seasons. The new animated Batman also appeared in *Batman Beyond: The Movie*, which came out in 1999.

The next Batman movie did not appear until 2005. *Batman Begins* tells the Caped Crusader's origin story once again. This time, the filmmaker was Christopher Nolan, and Christian Bale played Batman. And once again, the film was more like the serious stories by Frank Miller than the comic versions of Batman. In this movie, Batman begins his crime-fighting career battling Ra's al Ghul and the Scarecrow.

Christian Bale as Batman in *Batman Begins*

Heath Ledger as the Joker in *The Dark Knight*

Nolan and Bale teamed up to make two more Batman movies: *The Dark Knight* (2008) and *The Dark Knight Rises* (2012). In *The Dark Knight*, Batman once again fights the Joker. Heath Ledger played the grinning villain in a new and even scarier way than fans had ever seen him before.

In the last film, Batman faces Bane, who wants to destroy Gotham City with a powerful bomb.

These three movies once again proved how popular Batman was—even into the twenty-first century. People around the world rushed to see them, and together they made almost $2.5 billion! What could Batman do to top that? Fans were eager to find out what Batman adventures were still to come.

CHAPTER 9
Batman Lives!

Warner Bros. soon developed new stories for Batman fans. The 2014 TV show *Gotham* told the story of Bruce Wayne before he became Batman. Bruce meets James Gordon for the first time when he is still a police officer trying to find out who murdered Bruce's parents. By the fourth season, Bruce begins to wear a mask and fight crime, but he hasn't become Batman quite yet. He finally emerges as the super hero in the fifth and final season of the show.

While the show aired, Batman's teen years were explored in a novel for young readers. Marie Lu's book *Batman: Nightwalker* was published in 2017.

Batman appeared in yet another form in 2014—as a LEGO figure! *The LEGO Movie* features a number of animated characters made from the famous toy building blocks. In the movie, Batman helps Emmet and a crew of minifigures fight an evil businessman who is trying to take over the world. The actor Will Arnett provided the voice for Batman.

Will Arnett

The LEGO Movie won several awards as the best animated feature film of 2014. Its success led to *The LEGO Batman Movie* in 2017, with Batgirl and Robin joining Batman in a LEGO version of Gotham City. They face the Joker, who works with LEGO minifigures of monsters and bad guys from many different books and movies. These super villains included ferocious dinosaurs, a vampire, a mummy, and Lord Voldemort from the Harry Potter book series. Of course, Batman, Robin, and Batgirl save the city from destruction in the end.

Batman has played a role in Warner Bros.' new live-action movies featuring some of its other DC super heroes. In 2016, Batman and Superman appeared for the first time together in *Batman v Superman: Dawn of Justice*. In the movie, the two crime-fighting heroes become enemies. They finally realize, though, that they have a common enemy in Lex Luthor, and they must defeat him.

Playing Games with Batman

For Batman fans, 1986 was a big year. A British company created a Batman video game to play on personal computers. Three years later, the company released a game based on the 1989 movie *Batman*. In the decades since, Batman and some of the villains he battles have appeared in dozens of other video games.

But not every Batman game requires a computer or video game console. In 1991, the first Batman pinball game was sold. Players used two flippers to hit balls and try to earn points. In 2016, three different versions of a Batman pinball game, all based on the 1966 TV show, became available.

Ben Affleck played Batman in *Batman v Superman: Dawn of Justice* and again the next year in *Justice League.* Just as in the comics, a group of DC super heroes work as a team to fight evil.

What does the future hold for Batman? At this moment, DC writers and artists are creating more comics and graphic novels featuring the Caped Crusader. Fans can read some of the new stories and classic Batman comics online.

Warner Bros. has new films in the works with Batman as either the star or a key figure.

Batman has faced many challenges since Bob Kane created him with Bill Finger in 1939. Over the decades, some things have always remained true: Batman is a skilled detective and a smart super hero who will risk his life to fight the world's worst villains. And his fans will always be thrilled by his stories of good defeating evil.

Collecting Batman

Think you might like to buy a copy of *Detective No. 27*, which featured the first Batman story? In 1939 fans paid only ten cents for that comic. But today, it's worth more than $1 million!

Batman No. 1 sold at an auction for more than $500,000. A toy utility belt that was made when the 1966 *Batman* show went on the air has sold for over $16,000. And small metal Batmobiles can be worth several thousand dollars.

Bibliography

*Books for young readers

Brooker, Will. *Batman Unmasked: Analysing a Cultural Icon.*
London: Continuum, 2000.

Brooker, Will. *Hunting the Dark Knight: Twenty-First Century
Batman.* London: I. B. Tauris, 2012.

Daniels, Les. *Batman: The Complete History.* San Francisco:
Chronicle Books, 1999.

Greenberger, Robert. *The Essential Batman Encyclopedia.*
New York: Del Rey, 2008.

Kane, Bob, with Tom Andrae. *Batman & Me.* Forestville, CA:
Eclipse Books, 1989.

* Wallace, Daniel. *Batman: The World of the Dark Knight.*
New York: DK, 2012.

Websites

www.dccomics.com

www.1966batmobile.com